FIRST PEOPLES

THE YANOMAMI

OF SOUTH AMERICA

RAYA TAHAN

Lerner Publications Company • Minneapolis

**First American edition published in 2002
by Lerner Publications Company**

Published by arrangement with Times Editions

Copyright © 2002 by Times Media Private Limited

Lerner Publications Company
A division of Lerner Publishing Group
241 First Avenue North
Minneapolis, MN 55401 U.S.A.
Website address: www.lernerbooks.com

Series originated and designed by
Times Editions
An imprint of Times Media Private Limited
A member of the Times Publishing Group
1 New Industrial Road, Singapore 536196
Website address: www.timesone.com.sg/te

Series editors: Margaret J. Goldstein, Yumi Ng
Series designers: Tuck Loong, Lynn Chin
Series picture researcher: Susan Jane Manuel

Library of Congress Cataloging-in-Publication Data
Tahan, Raya.
The Yanomami of South America / by Raya Tahan.
p. cm. — (First peoples)
Includes bibliographical references and index.
ISBN 0-8225-4851-8 (lib. bdg. : alk. paper)
1. Yanomamo Indians—History—Juvenile literature. 2. Yanomamo
Indians—Social conditions—Juvenile literature. 3. Indians,
Treatment of—Brazil—Juvenile literature. [1. Yanomamo Indians.
2. Indians of South America—Amazon River Region.] I. Title. II. Series.
F2520.1.Y3 T35   2002
981.004'98—dc21   00-013112

Printed in Singapore
Bound in the United States of America

1 2 3 4 5 6—0S—07 06 05 04 03 02

CONTENTS

THE YANOMAMI OF SOUTH AMERICA

The Yanomami are a large group of native people living in northern Brazil and southern Venezuela in South America. The Yanomami population of about twenty thousand is divided about equally between the two countries. The Yanomami are the world's largest native group still living a traditional lifestyle—living much like their ancestors did. The Yanomami live in the Amazon jungle, the world's largest tropical rain forest. They have lived there for thousands of years, sharing the forest with plants and animals. Yanomami children learn early how to hunt, fish, and plant gardens. They also learn which plants are useful as medicine. Some of these children know more about the rain forest than scientists who have studied the area for many years.

Villages in the Rain Forest

The Yanomami live in small villages, each with somewhere between 40 and 150 people. About 200 to 350 Yanomami villages are scattered widely throughout their territory. For the most part, people in the villages still live as their ancestors did many years before them. They don't drive cars or go to school. Everything they need to survive—including food, medicine, and clothing—comes from the forest. In recent years, some Yanomami groups have started to live more like people in big cities do, however.

Neighbors in the Amazon

Besides the Yanomami, about 170 other native groups live in the Amazon region. Each of these cultures is unique, with its own language, religion, beliefs, and lifestyles. The Yekuana people live near the Yanomami in the forests of Brazil. In fact, some Yekuana have married Yanomami.

THE RAIN FOREST IN DANGER

More and more outsiders are coming to the isolated rain forest of South America. These outsiders are cutting down and changing the forest. But for thousands of years, the forest has provided the Yanomami with everything they need. As the forest disappears, the Yanomami (*right*) are struggling to keep their traditional ways alive.

THE WORLD'S LARGEST RIVER

The Amazon River in South America is just over 4,000 miles (6,400 kilometers) long. In some places, it is 300 feet (91 meters) deep and 9 miles (15 kilometers) wide. The Nile River in Africa is about 100 miles (160 kilometers) longer. But the Amazon is still considered the world's largest river because it pours the most water into the sea. Every second, about 7 million cubic feet (198,000 cubic meters) of water flow from the Amazon into the Atlantic Ocean. That's enough water to fill up Lake Ontario in three hours.

Left: An Amazon tributary runs through the Andes Mountains in Bolivia.

Snaking to the Sea

The Amazon River coils across South America like a snake. The Amazon begins as a network of streams in the Andes Mountains of Peru. These streams flow together, creating a small river at first. Eventually, many more streams and small rivers, called tributaries, flow into the Amazon, like veins in a leaf. The Amazon has more than ten thousand tributaries. As it flows east, the river gets bigger until it empties into the Atlantic Ocean at the Brazilian coast. The place where a river empties into the ocean is called its mouth. The mouth of the Amazon is 205 miles (330 kilometers) across.

Water, Water, Everywhere

The lands around a big river and all the smaller rivers that drain into it are called a river basin. The Amazon River basin is as big as Australia. It includes parts of six countries: Peru, Venezuela, Ecuador, Colombia, Bolivia, and Brazil. The Yanomami live in just a small part of the river basin. More than 100 inches (2.5 meters) of rain fall every year in the Amazon River basin, making it one of the wettest regions in the world.

Above: Rain clouds loom over the rain forest.

Below: Two men in Brazil navigate the waters of the Amazon River.

WHAT'S IN A NAME

Because the Amazon looks like a snake twisting its away across South America, the ancient Peruvians called it Amaru-Mayu, which means "Great Serpent—Mother of Men." When the first European explorers arrived in the South American rain forest, they claimed they had met a group of fierce women warriors. Francisco de Orellana, one of the explorers, thought they had met the Amazons—a race of women warriors that was popular in Greek myths. He called the river that ran along the forest the Amazon River.

RAIN FOREST PLANTS

The Amazon rain forest is full of mysterious and exotic plants. Scientists believe that more than fifty thousand kinds of plants and trees grow here. Nowhere else on earth has such a wide variety of plant life. The Amazon rain forest is located at the equator, an imaginary line that runs around the middle of the globe. Temperatures at the equator are very high. The average daytime temperature in the Amazon region is about 80 degrees Fahrenheit (26 degrees Celsius). The plants that grow here thrive in hot weather.

A Colorful Garden

If you were to walk for a couple of miles in the United States, you would probably see fewer than ten kinds of trees. If you walked that far in the Amazon rain forest, you would see around two hundred different types of trees, in all different shades of green. Some trees in the Amazon stand as tall as 200 feet (61 meters). Colorful flowering plants called orchids grow high on the tops of the tree branches.

Left: The dish-shaped leaves of giant water lilies catch rainwater.

Rainy Days

In the Amazon region, it rains heavily on most days during the rainy season, which lasts from April to November. Much less rain falls during the dry season—from December to March. But these months can still be rainy. The trees of the forest soak up a lot of rainwater through their roots. The water moves from the roots to the tree trunks and then into the leaves. The leaves give off moisture into the air. Because of all the moisture in the air, the rain forest is very humid—wet and sticky.

Left: The bright-red heliconia hangs down from a tree branch.

Valuable Products

The plants of the Amazon provide people with fruits, nuts, and fragrant oils. Loggers cut down and sell the trees of the rain forest, including mahogany and rosewood trees, because the wood is very valuable. About 25 percent of our medicines come from rain forest plants. Scientists believe that many more medicines are yet to be discovered in the forest. The Yanomami and other Amazon peoples have known for many centuries about the healing power of certain plants.

Above: The seeds of the cacao tree are used to make chocolate.

DIFFERENT KINDS OF SEASONS

The Amazon rain forest lies at the equator. A broad area on either side of the equator is called the tropics, or tropical zone. Tropical places get lots of sunshine all year long. They don't have winter, spring, summer, and fall like many places in the United States do. Instead, many tropical places have a wet season and a dry season. In the Amazon, the wet season lasts from April to November. The dry season lasts from December to March. It is very hot in the Amazon during the daytime. The air cools off a little bit at night.

RAIN FOREST ANIMALS

The Amazon basin is home to thousands of animals. Monkeys, jaguars, and parrots all live in the rain forest. Three thousand varieties of fish and millions of kinds of insects are found here. The plants and animals of the forest depend on each other. Plants serve as food for the animals. Animals help the plants by spreading seeds and enriching the soil with their droppings.

On Dry Land

Some unusual land animals live in the rain forest. The tapir looks a little bit like a pig, and it can weigh up to 800 pounds (363 kilograms). The Yanomami often hunt tapirs for food. The anteater is a tropical mammal that uses its long snout and long tongue to feed on insects. Poisonous coral snakes, bright green iguanas, and tree frogs also live here.

Right: The jaguar is an animal native to the Amazon rain forest.

In the Water

The waters of the Amazon are full of animals, such as dolphins, turtles, and alligators. The pirarucu is a large freshwater fish—it can weigh up to 325 pounds (147 kilograms). The huge anaconda snake swims in the water and slides over land. Popular aquarium fish, such as silver carp and neon tetras, also swim in the waters of the Amazon.

In the Air

Thousands of kinds of birds live in the Amazon River basin. In fact, about one-fifth of all the bird species in the world can be found here. The birds of the Amazon include colorful parrots, hummingbirds, macaws, and toucans with black feathers and large colorful beaks. Giant butterflies flutter through the air, while vampire bats and fruit bats fly among the trees.

Above: The toucan is one of the many species of birds found in the rain forest.

Crawling with Insects

Millions of types of insects live in the Amazon basin, including beetles, bees, and spiders. One large fuzzy spider called a tarantula has large fangs that it uses to bite and poison its prey. Fleas live in the rain forest, as do small ticks that feed on the blood of other animals. Thousands of kinds of ants live in the rain forest, too.

Left: A graceful and colorful butterfly in the forest near the Negro River in Brazil.

A MONSTER OF A RODENT

Weighing up to 140 pounds (64 kilograms), the capybara (*right*) is the largest rodent in the world. The capybara looks like a huge guinea pig, but with tough skin, coarse red or brown fur, webbed toes, and long back legs. Scientists think the huge rodent is probably related to the hippopotamus. Capybaras live near rivers, lakes, and swamps because they like to be near water. They communicate with each other by making squeaks, whistles, and grunts. They eat leaves, seeds, and sugarcane from Yanomami fields.

UNKNOWN BEGINNINGS

We know very little about the history of the Yanomami. They did not have a written language until recently, so we can't study their past in history books. They do not build permanent houses, so we can't study their ancient buildings. Unlike many native groups, the Yanomami do not make tools out of stone. Instead they use wood, bones, feathers, and other materials that decay over time. So scientists cannot dig in the soil for old tools that might teach them about ancient Yanomami culture.

Crossing Continents

Many experts believe the Yanomami and other native peoples in the Americas descend from a group of Asian people who traveled to North America, perhaps as early as twenty thousand years ago. The people came from northern Asia to Alaska in North America, over a strip of land that has since been covered by the sea. The people then headed down through North and Central America and into South America. Generation after generation, they moved farther south, closer to the Amazon River.

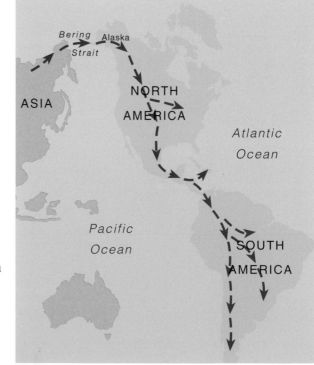

Above: The Yanomami make their tools out of materials found in the rain forest.

Changing Climate

Every year the earth's climate, or weather pattern, changes a tiny bit—so little that we usually can't notice it. But when scientists study climate over many years, they can see big changes. The climate in the Amazon region was dry thousands of years ago when the ancestors of the Yanomami arrived there. But it grew wetter every century, making the region so wet and sticky that skeletons and other fossils (animal and plant remains) decayed quickly. Without fossils to study, scientists have a hard time learning about people who lived in the Amazon many years ago.

Other Ancestors

Some anthropologists (scientists who study human cultures) believe that the ancestors of the Yanomami lived on islands in the Caribbean Sea near Florida before coming to South America. According to one theory, about fifteen thousand years ago, people left the Caribbean by boat and then walked through Central and South America. It is difficult to walk through this mountainous region.

NO BONES ABOUT IT

Decay is one reason that anthropologists cannot find ancient skeletons of Yanomami people. Another reason is that the Yanomami don't bury people after they die. Instead, most Yanomami cremate, or burn, dead bodies. They mix the ashes with banana juice. The dead person's closest family members drink the mixture at the funeral ceremony.

CONTACT WITH OUTSIDERS

Euuropean explorers first came to the Amazon region in the late 1400s. They met many native groups. But they did not meet any Yanomami. The Yanomami live deep in the rain forest jungle. Europeans did not have the skills to travel through the jungle. The Yanomami did not often leave the forest to explore the outside world. So the two groups had very little contact.

First Contact

In the late 1700s, European explorers in South America began hearing rumors of a fierce tribe that may have been the Yanomami. In 1799, Alexander von Humboldt, a German explorer, said that his expedition had met a group of Yanomami. The explorers said that the group seemed warlike. But because they did not live with the Yanomami, the explorers didn't know that the group is mostly peaceful.

Below: A group of men travel on foot to attend a feast at a nearby village.

Above: Missionaries often provide the Yanomami with medicines.

Rubber Boom

Many rubber trees grow in the Amazon. The demand for rubber brought more outsiders to the region in the late 1800s and early 1900s. During this "rubber boom," foreign workers cut into the bark of the trees, caught the dripping sap in buckets, and heated it to make solid rubber. The rubber was used to make shoes and other items sold in Europe and the United States. The Yanomami gave food to the rubber workers in exchange for knives and tools.

DISAPPEARING TREES

Since the 1950s, cattle ranchers have cut down trees (*below*) in the rain forest to raise cattle in the fields. Loggers have also cut down trees and sold the wood to factories. But many people believe that the rain forests should not be cut down at all. The trees provide a home for plants, animals, and native peoples. The trees also absorb carbon dioxide and give off oxygen. In this way, the trees help maintain a balanced climate.

Visiting Missionaries

In the 1950s, Christian missionaries from North America came to the Amazon to convert the Yanomami to Christianity. The missionaries built houses and stayed for many years, sometimes for the rest of their lives. For the most part, they were not able to convince the Yanomami to take up Christianity. But in many villages, the two groups became friends.

GOLD RUSH

In the 1980s, gold was discovered on Yanomami lands in Brazil. Thousands of miners, eager to become rich, came to dig up the gold and sell it. The gold rush of the 1980s brought major problems and deadly diseases into the rain forest.

Animals Scared Away

The miners used high-pressure water hoses to loosen the soil along riverbanks. They pumped the soil into machines to find the gold inside. The hoses and pumps made loud noises, which frightened away the animals that the Yanomami normally hunted. The hoses made the rivers muddy and killed the fish. The Yanomami could no longer fish or hunt as usual. They grew hungry and unhealthy.

Below: Miners dig up gold in Brazil.

Poison Mercury

The miners used a metal called mercury to find bits of gold stuck to soil and rocks. During this process, liquid mercury spilled into rivers or evaporated into the air. Mercury is very poisonous. People who breathe in mercury or eat fish that have absorbed mercury can develop cancer, skin problems, or pneumonia. Some Yanomami people, including many children, died from mercury poisoning during the gold rush.

Right: A gold miner holds liquid mercury in his hand.

Outside Diseases

Some of the miners were sick with measles, malaria, or tuberculosis. Most of them were able to recover from these diseases because their bodies had immunity, or built-in protection, against them. But the Yanomami did not have immunity to the diseases because their ancestors had never been exposed to them. Mosquitoes spread malaria by biting miners who had the disease, then biting healthy Yanomami. In the late 1980s, almost one out of every five Yanomami in Brazil died from diseases brought by outsiders.

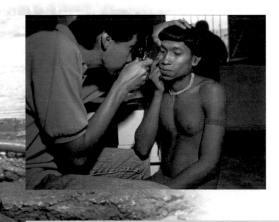

Left: A Brazilian doctor examines a Yanomami.

THE WORLD HELPS

People from around the world heard about the problems created by the gold miners and tried to help the Yanomami. Many international organizations, including the United Nations, and the Brazilian, German, and British governments, provided medical care to the Yanomami. The Brazilian government created a 40,000-square-mile (104,000-square-kilometer) reserve in northern Brazil, setting aside the land for the Yanomami only. Some gold miners break the rules and go into the reserve. The Yanomami who live there still suffer from problems brought by the outsiders.

MORE MODERN-DAY THREATS

The Yanomami do not believe that land can be owned by anybody. They believe that people share the land with animals and plants. But many outsiders who come to the rain forest do not share these beliefs. Human activities like mining, logging, farming, cattle ranching, and building highways and dams have damaged the jungle.

Left: The Itaipu Dam creates electricity for southern Brazil.

Dam Building

Dams are giant structures that use the power of rushing water to generate electricity. But dams can also change the natural course of rivers and flood big fields. Trees can't live in the flooded fields. Animals also die or move away from the flooded regions. Many people want to dam the tributaries of the Amazon River. But these dams would hurt the area's plants and animals. The dams would also hurt people such as the Yanomami who rely on the plants and animals for food.

Road Building

More and more people are moving into the forest to build farms and ranches and to cut down trees. The farmers and loggers travel by car and truck, so they must build roads through the forest. They cut down and burn trees and run bulldozers over the land. Animals get scared and run away when they see fires and hear loud engines. When the Yanomami go hunting, they find fewer and fewer animals. Without animals to hunt, the people go hungry.

Above: Brazilian ranchers clear the forest for cattle ranching.

Violence in the Rain Forest

Some outsiders move into the rain forest to find gold or to chop down trees. They end up making friends with the villagers. But many other outsiders do not like the Yanomami. They think the native people are standing in the way of their search for gold and trees. Sometimes this attitude leads to violence. Some miners, who are more powerful than the natives because they have guns, have murdered some Yanomami people. As an act of revenge, the Yanomami have also responded with murder on a few occasions.

WORKING TOGETHER

In their everyday life, the Yanomami do not use money. Everyone in the village does a job. Groups of people build houses, go hunting, and do other jobs together. Yanomami life is difficult and involves hard work. In recent years, however, some villagers have learned about money from outsiders. Villagers who live near missionary posts, for example, do odd jobs at the posts in exchange for money. Some villagers have started to mine gold for themselves, which they sell to outsiders. With the money they earn, the Yanomami buy factory-made goods from the city.

Below: Yanomami men at work in their vegetable garden

Fishing and Hunting

It's very important for Yanomami men to be good hunters. They earn respect and honor by providing meat for their families. Using bows and arrows, they hunt deer, tapirs, birds, and other wild animals. Women catch fish by moving handwoven baskets through streams. Men catch fish with lines and hooks or by shooting them with poisoned arrows.

Left: A hunter carries his catch of the day.

Farming

Every Yanomami village has a garden containing tropical fruits and vegetables such as papayas, sugarcanc, bananas, yams, sweet potatoes, and rasha, a deep-red fruit that grows on palm trees. People also grow plantains, a type of banana. They use big knives called machetes to cut the fruit once it is big enough to eat. Plantains are served at many meals. They're usually roasted and eaten hot. People often mash bananas with water to make a drink or a soft baby food. They eat manioc, a root vegetable that looks like a big, long potato. People sometimes bake manioc into bread over a campfire.

Gathering Wild Plants

The Yanomami also gather many foods that grow wild in the forest. They pick bacaba, a purple fruit the size of a marble. It grows on palm trees, and its juice is used in making a delicious drink. Other foods of the jungle include pineapples, Brazil nuts, avocados, and a sweet red berry called a hajuk.

CARRYING FIREWOOD

Gathering firewood is an important job that Yanomami women and girls (*right*) perform daily. Every day, groups of women chop up logs from fallen trees and carry the wood back home. Wood fires keep houses warm at night and cook the meat from each day's hunt. People start fires by rubbing sticks together, creating heat and then a flame.

JUNGLE TREK

The Yanomami do not spend their entire lives in one place. They are seminomadic, which means they sometimes move and sometimes live in the same place for a long time. Certain villages might stay in the same place for ten years. Other villages might move every two years. The Yanomami travel on foot. They camp in the forest at night and walk during the day.

Moving the Village

Why do the Yanomami travel? If their gardens will no longer grow vegetables, their hunting grounds run out of animals, or their houses become infested with insects, the whole village travels to find a new place to live. The rain forest is very big. However, finding a new home is not quite as easy as it used to be. Now that so much forest has been cleared and so many rivers have been polluted, some Yanomami must travel a bit farther to find a good spot to build a new house.

Below: Yanomami men build a temporary hut during a jungle trek.

Travel Conditions

The Yanomami prefer to travel during the dry season. During the rainy season, the trails through the forest are full of water and mud. Walking is difficult. But even during the dry season, walking through the jungle is very hard. Thorny bushes and vines are common. The Yanomami don't wear shoes or much clothing. So thorns might scratch them or stick in their feet.

Left: A Yanomami woman uses a giant leaf as a shelter from the rain.

Visiting Villages

The Yanomami travel to visit friends and relatives in other villages. Depending on where the villages are located, the walk might take a few hours or many days. Often, an entire village will walk together. This kind of journey takes twice as long as a trip made by just a few people because elderly people and women carrying babies cannot walk very quickly.

FIRST IN LINE

When the Yanomami travel, they walk single file, in a long line (*right*). They walk cautiously and know how to spot dangerous animals. Snakes usually bite the first person who disturbs them. Walking in the front of the line is reserved for the bravest person, usually a good hunter. He has to warn the rest of the group of any dangers on the trail.

A HOUSE FOR THE PEOPLE

In most Yanomami villages, people build one big round hut, about 100 feet (31 meters) wide. It's called a *shabono*, or a *yāno*, and the whole village—dozens of people—lives inside. In the middle is a big open plaza, where children play and adults perform rituals. The Yanomami build shabonos using tree trunks, vines, palm leaves, and other rain forest plants. Each family builds its own section of the shabono, called a *nano*.

Below: The shabono, or communal house, is home to one entire village.

Sleeping in Mid-Air

The Yanomami sleep in hammocks that hang near the fire. Children sleep with their mothers until they turn five or until they have a younger brother or sister. Then they get their own hammocks. The most comfortable hammocks are made of cotton, which is grown in people's gardens. Some people sleep on hammocks made of vines.

Left: A Yanomami family gathers at their nano.

Outside Influences

Yanomami people who have had contact with outsiders have adopted foreign building styles. Some people have built square huts, like the houses found in Europe and the United States.

Right: A house built with factory-made materials

Life in a Nano

Nanos are small, and much of the space is taken up by a hearth, an open fire used for cooking and heating. Families usually hang baskets, water containers made from gourds, and bunches of plantains and bananas from the roof of the nano. Because all the nanos are connected inside the shabono, people can see, hear, and smell almost everything going on in their village.

GOING BUGGY

After two or three years, the roof of a shabono becomes leaky and its walls get infested with cockroaches, crickets, lice, spiders, and other insects. When people brush against the walls, cockroaches fall from the roof and scurry across the floor. That's when the community moves out of the shabono and builds a new one. They burn the old shabono to the ground to kill the insects living there.

ONE DAY AT A TIME

Yanomami people typically wake up when they hear a baby crying or feel the chilly morning air. Men leave early to go hunting for game. By the time the sun comes up, women are roasting plantains over the fire and heating up leftover meat from the last night's dinner. After breakfast, people work in the garden, clearing away weeds and planting new crops. By 11 A.M., the sun is hot and the air is humid, which makes working outside difficult.

Below: Men butcher a giant anteater caught during the day's hunt.

More Work in the Afternoon

By mid-afternoon, people are off again to collect water from the river, play in the forest, or hunt. When the sun starts to set at night, each family gets ready for dinner. The evening meal is the biggest one of the day. It usually consists of meat from the day's hunt, plus fruit and vegetables from the garden and the rain forest.

Left: Women bake flat breads made from manioc flour.

Above: Each person sleeps in his or her own hammock.

Good Night

Before going to sleep, everyone wipes dirt off their feet and climbs into their hammocks. To keep warm at night, they keep their hammocks close to the fire. Someone has to add wood and stir the fire throughout the night to keep it burning. Sometimes it's hard to fall asleep because the shabono is noisy with babies crying, sick people coughing, and friends telling stories.

COMMUNITY LEADERS

The Yanomami do not have a ruler who enforces the law. However, most villages have a headman, who is thought to be the smartest or most charming man. He is considered equal to everybody else in the village and must do all the same chores. He also does an extra job: he must keep order within the village and communicate with other villages.

TRADITIONS AND TRANSFORMATIONS

Some parts of Yanomami culture have stayed the same for many generations. Other parts of the culture are changing every day. In recent years, the Yanomami have had contact with people from modern countries such as the United States. As a result, many traditions are changing. For instance, the Yanomami sometimes use factory-made containers and wear modern clothing.

Below: Yanomami women of Venezuela wash vegetables in the river.

New Containers

Traditionally, the Yanomami wove baskets from palm leaves or tree bark. They stored food and other items in these baskets. Recently, outsiders have brought factory-made goods to the forest. The Yanomami like to trade with foreigners for aluminum pots.

Above: Traditional and modern Yanomami tools

High Honey

One thing that has not changed about the Yanomami is their love of honey. When somebody finds a beehive high up in a tree, a man will climb up, holding burning leaves in one hand to make the bees fly away. Then he will chop up the hive, and the people below will pick it up and eat the honey inside. They'll take leftovers back to the village.

Spinning Cotton

To make hammocks and clothing, Yanomami women grow cotton in their gardens. They pick the cotton, dry it in the sun, and pull the white fluff apart from the black seeds. Then they gather up a big ball of white fluff and run it through a spindle, or a weaving frame, made of two large poles.

Left: A boy eats honey from a hive found in a fallen tree.

DOGGONE GOOD PETS

The Yanomami love to keep pets. In some villages, every household has a dog. Children love to play with dogs, and men take them hunting. Sometimes the Yanomami find baby monkeys or baby parrots alone in the rain forest, without their mothers. People take these babies back to the villages and keep them as pets. The Yanomami also eat monkeys and parrots that they have hunted and killed. But they would never eat their pets.

CONFLICT IN THE VILLAGES

The Yanomami are mostly friendly toward others. They visit neighboring villages to hold parties and trade household items. But, just like people in all societies, the Yanomami sometimes fight among themselves. In the past, Yanomami raiders attacked other villages, hurting and even killing people. But since the 1980s, miners and other outsiders have become the biggest enemies of the Yanomami. Some villages have stopped fighting with each other and have teamed up to fight against outsiders.

Below: Yanomami men bearing weapons to be used in a dance walk to a nearby village.

Kidnapping and Revenge

In the past, Yanomami raiders sometimes attacked neighboring villages to kidnap one another's wives. Because they were scared of being kidnapped, women did their chores in groups. If a woman was kidnapped, the men from her home village would go to the kidnappers' village to recapture her and to take revenge upon her kidnappers. In recent times, kidnapping has become rare.

Left: Women usually do chores in groups.

Old and New Weapons

The Yanomami used to fight one another with clubs, bows, arrows, and spears. They made these weapons by hand, using wood, bone, and other items they found in the rain forest. But Yanomami weapons have changed a lot. By trading with outsiders, the Yanomami have obtained deadlier weapons such as guns, axes, and hatchets.

Below: Arrowheads made by Venezuelan Yanomami

MISTAKEN IDENTITY

When one American anthropologist first met the Yanomami in the 1960s, he saw that they sometimes fought with one another. He mistakenly called them "the fierce people" because he did not understand their culture. Since then, many other anthropologists have visited the Yanomami and have spent decades living in their villages. These people disagree with the old "fierce" description. They say that the Yanomami mostly live together in harmony.

CHILDREN'S LIVES

Most Yanomami children do not go to school. They learn about their world by watching and listening to elders and by playing in the jungle. Children swim on hot days, swinging from vines and dropping into the cool water. Young boys hunt lizards with miniature bows and arrows. By the time they are fourteen years old, Yanomami children are experts on the rain forest.

A Baby's Life

For the first couple of years, mothers take their babies with them when they go out to work. They carry the babies in slings made from tree bark. Mothers make soft baby food by squishing up fruit or meat and mixing it with water. Babies learn to stand and walk by holding onto sticks poked into the ground.

Above: Yanomami babies rarely leave their mothers' side during their early years.

Below: A Yanomami boy makes a fire for roasting meat.

Time to Work

Yanomami boys sometimes help with building tools or go on hunting trips with their fathers, uncles, and older brothers. But mostly, until they are twenty years old, boys are free to play with their friends all day. Yanomami girls begin working at a much younger age. When they are about nine years old, girls begin to baby-sit their younger brothers and sisters and help their mothers cook.

Kidding Around

Like children everywhere, Yanomami children like to play games. In a game called Get the Bee, boys and girls catch live bees, tie strings to the bees' bodies, and hold onto the strings while the bees fly away. Since Yanomami children grow up among the animals and insects of the rain forest, they know how to handle the bees without getting stung. In another game, children gather leaves from the forest and use the leaves to make a dummy that looks like a person. They walk away from the dummy and travel around the forest on a pretend hunting trip. When they find the dummy, they shoot it full of arrows.

Below: Yanomami boys play with bows and arrows.

FOOD TABOOS

The Yanomami believe many actions are taboo, or forbidden, because they can cause sickness, harm, or even death. There are many taboos about food. For instance, a pregnant woman must not eat fish, because the Yanomami believe that the spines will prick the woman's baby. Once the child is born, and until he or she begins to walk, the child must not eat parrot meat. Otherwise, the child will become ill. The Yanomami also believe that if a child eats monkey's meat, his or her tongue will rot.

PERFORMING ARTS

The Yanomami express themselves artistically by singing and dancing. Music is also a way to teach others. For example, some songs tell how the world was formed. Other songs are long myths that elders sing to children while they dance and play. Once the children grow up, they will sing the same songs and teach their children the old stories.

Songs and Music

The Yanomami use songs to pass along information about religion, history, or activities. A song leader might sing a song about hunting. Then villagers will sing the leader's words back to him while they all dance in a big circle. The singing and dancing usually start after dinner and can last for hours. The Yanomami do not play drums, guitars, or other big musical instruments. They sometimes play flutes made from bamboo or animal bones.

Below: Yanomami boys and men perform a traditional dance.

Left: Yanomami men listen to a storyteller's tale.

Storytelling

Yanomami men love to tell folktales at nighttime. They use big hand gestures, funny voices, and facial expressions to entertain their audience. A popular story is about Iwariwa, the spirit who discovered fire. In this story, the fire came from a lightning strike in the forest. Iwariwa used to be the only one who had the fire, and he kept it inside his body. One day, somebody tricked him into laughing, and the fire escaped from his mouth. Then Iwariwa turned into an alligator.

CHANTING

When the people of one Yanomami village visit another village for a special occasion, the two groups like to watch a ritual of chanting. In this practice, men tell news, talk about problems, and discuss trading items with each other. The ritual starts when one man begins chanting softly and asks another man to repeat his words. They take turns saying sentences and mimicking each other. Sometimes they rhyme, scream, or make other noises. The chanting can last all night, until the sun comes up.

YANOMAMI FASHION

Because the weather is very warm and humid in the tropical rain forest, the Yanomami do not need clothes to protect them from snow and frostbite. Many Yanomami wear only loincloths that look like little aprons. They also wear strings of cotton tied around their wrists, ankles, knees, and chests. Some villages have had a lot of contact with missionaries, gold miners, and other outsiders. In these villages, people sometimes wear shorts, T-shirts, and dresses that come from the city.

Clothing for Women and Girls

The traditional clothing for a Yanomami woman or girl is a cotton loincloth tied low around the hips like an apron. Sometimes the loincloth is dyed bright red and the bottom is fringed for decoration. Girls also like to wear strings of cotton tied in different designs. They tie these beautiful creations around their arms, waists, and necks. Women and girls also pierce their earlobes, noses, and lower lips and put sticks called arrow canes through the piercings. They also wear flowers in their ears and tied onto cotton armbands.

Left: These Yanomami women wear a mixture of modern and traditional clothes.

Jewelry and Decorations

The Yanomami make lots of beautiful jewelry from items found in the rain forest. They often decorate their bodies with strings of seeds, animal teeth, and even the bones of dead stingrays. They wear the jewelry tied around their upper arms, ankles, necks, waists, chests—almost anywhere.

Left: A young Yanomami woman paints her body and face for a festival.

Men's Clothing

Besides loincloths, Yanomami men and boys usually do not wear much clothing. But they love to decorate themselves with large, colorful feathers and the pelts of parrots, toucans, macaws, and other tropical birds. They make headdresses out of the feathers and tie feathers to their arms.

Below: A Yanomami man wearing festival clothing

BODY PAINT

The Yanomami like to decorate themselves with body paint for special occasions (*above*). The designs are based on jungle plants and animals. The Yanomami usually put red paint on their faces. The red paint provides decoration and also prevents sunburn, wards off insects, and smells good. Red paint comes from the seeds of the annatto tree. Black paint comes from the fruit of the genipap tree or from a mix of annatto seeds and ashes.

YANOMAMI LANGUAGES

Yanomami people speak different languages, depending on where they live. The languages are Ninam, Sanuma, Yanomamo, Yanomam, and Aica. Each language has its own special rules, but the languages are similar to each other. People who speak different Yanomami languages can often understand one another. Most Yanomami people do not read or write or look up words in the dictionary. Instead, they have very good memories and learn a lot of words by heart.

Above: Two Yanomami men exchange stories during a festival.

Learn to Speak Yanomam

Here is a chart of some Yanomam words and phrases. The first column shows the Yanomam word, the second column shows how to pronounce the word, and the third column shows what it means in English. (The syllable written in all capital letters is the syllable that gets stressed in speaking.)

Yanomam	Pronunciation	English
ara a	AH-rah ah	one macaw
awe	aw-EH	yes
iro	EE-roh	a band of howler monkeys
koratha	koh-RAH-tah	a bunch of bananas
ma	MAH	no
oko a	OH-koh ah	a freshwater crab
pei mamo	BAY MAH-moh	eye
waka a	WAH-kah ah	a giant armadillo

SPEAKING WITHOUT WORDS

The Yanomami sometimes communicate with facial expressions and hand gestures. For instance, a man who is disgusted by something he has just heard will lock eyes with the speaker, move his head and eyes away, and then spit on the ground. To signal that he understands, he will raise and lower his eyebrows or breathe quickly with his mouth. Instead of plugging their noses with a thumb and index finger, like we do in North America, the Yanomami stick a finger into each nostril to show that they smell something stinky.

Names and Numbers

The Yanomami have names for only five colors: white, black, blue-green, yellow, and red. The word for white also means "clean," the word for black also means "dark," and the word for red also means "fire" and "ripe." Large numbers are not very important to the Yanomami. They do not know or care about their ages, and they don't do math. "One," "two," and "more than two" are the only numbers in the Yanomami languages. The Yanomami do not have a general word for "monkey," but they do have specific words for the five species of monkeys that live near them in the rain forest.

Below: A Yanomami looks at a book about his people.

SHAMANS AND SPIRITS

Shamans are found in many societies around the world. They are important people who talk with spirits and use magic to heal the sick. Most Yanomami villages have many highly respected shamans. Any boy can become a shaman. But he must go through a difficult training period that usually starts when he is fifteen and lasts many years. During the beginning of his training period, the boy eats almost nothing as a way to purify himself. Older shamans teach him chants, dances, and mysteries. Eventually, the men decide that the spirits have accepted the boy into their world, and he becomes a shaman.

Right: A Yanomami shaman speaks to a spirit during a ceremony.

Spirits of the Living

The Yanomami believe that every living person has a spirit that lives in the forest. This spirit takes the form of an otter, eagle, monkey, jaguar, or other animal. A good spirit keeps the person healthy and helps hunters find animals. If a person's spirit gets lost, he or she will become sick. A shaman must find the spirit for the person to become healthy again. People have two other spirits inside their bodies. One spirit lives in the liver. The other spirit lives inside a person's chest.

Spirits of the Dead

The Yanomami believe that when someone dies, part of his or her soul may turn into a fierce spirit that has teeth like a jaguar and bright, glowing eyes. This kind of spirit wanders the jungle, attacks travelers at night, and sometimes comes to the village of the dead person to harm those who are still living there. Only shamans can actually see this kind of spirit and scare it away.

Left: A spider monkey

SPIRITS AND CHILDREN

The Yanomami believe that children are more likely than adults to be bothered by evil spirits. That's because children's souls are not fixed inside their bodies and can spill out at any time, especially through the mouth when a child cries. Shamans (*below*) are religious leaders who protect children from curses and evil spirits.

Tiny Spirits

A shaman's body is home to *hekula*, tiny black spirits that have the power to heal. When somebody is sick, the shaman tells the spirits inside his body to get out and help the patient recover. These spirits look like different animals, and each type has a certain power. The spirits that look like spider monkeys can cure problems with the eyes, liver, legs, and arms. Besides helping sick people, shamans ask the hekula to bring game to the hunters. Shamans also use their power to harm people they dislike.

MYTHS AND THE COSMOS

Myths are sacred stories that help people understand the world around them and how it came to be. The Yanomami have many interesting myths about the creation of the first human beings and the shape of the universe. These stories have been passed down by Yanomami storytellers from generation to generation.

A Four-Layered Universe

For the Yanomami, the universe is made up of four layers. Some people believe that nobody lives in the top layer. Others believe that the top layer is full of happy people and rich hunting grounds. The next layer down is a beautiful place where the souls of dead people go to continue living. When Yanomami people look up and see the sky, they believe they are looking at the underside of this layer. The third layer is right here on earth. The bottom layer is a strange place. Some Yanomami believe it is the home of people who fell from the sky layer, passed through the earth layer, and landed at the bottom. There are no animals in this layer, so the people there eat each other.

Above: Low clouds hang above the rain forest.

The First Beings

According to a Yanomami myth, the first human beings were part people and part spirits. These beings shot the moon in the belly, and the moon's blood dripped down to earth, turning them into men. Where the blood was thickest, the men were fierce and they killed one another. Where the blood had mixed with water, the men were gentler and survived.

The Story of Foreigners

The Yanomami believe that their ancestors were the first human beings in the universe. One day, there was a great flood. Some Yanomami escaped by holding onto logs and floating down the river. They were not seen for many years. But a spirit fished them out of the river and wrung them out, which made them look different and speak a different language. Many years later, these people returned to their villages, floating in on logs in the shape of canoes. These people were explorers and other foreigners.

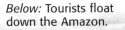
Below: Tourists float down the Amazon.

DOGS IN THE JUNGLE

Some scientists believe that European explorers brought dogs with them when they came to South America hundreds of years ago. The Yanomami believe that dogs have always lived in the jungle, but that they used to live away from people. But the Yanomami wanted the dogs (*above*) to help them hunt tapirs, so people tied meat onto ropes and threw the meat near the dogs. When they bit into the meat, people pulled the ropes, dragging the dogs into their villages.

YÃIMO—THE YANOMAMI FUNERAL

For the Yanomami, the death of a friend or family member is very sad. But the funeral can be joyful. While the Yanomami mourn somebody's death, they also celebrate the gift of life. The *yãimo*, or funeral, is a big ceremony with dancing and feasting. Guests come from other villages to join in the ceremony. This feast lasts for several days.

Below: Yanomami children perform a dance during a yãimo.

The Ceremony

Guests arrive with gifts for their hosts. Then the ceremony begins with joyful singing and dancing. A group of people stand in a circle, watching while others dance in the middle. The dancers wear their best clothing and jewelry—white feathers in their hair, red feathers tied to their arms, red and black paint on their faces, shells and metal pieces dangling from their aprons. People will continue to eat, drink, and dance all night long.

Left: Yanomami men drink manioc juice during a yāimo.

Trading at the Yāimo

One of the most important parts of the yāimo is trading items with members of the visiting villages. This trading happens quickly, with two men talking and chanting very rapidly. They squat in front of everybody else, describing which items they want and which items they are willing to give away as part of a deal.

DRINKING THE ASHES

The funeral ceremony cannot end until the family members of the dead person perform an important ritual. This ritual is the most serious part of the yāimo. Months before the funeral, the dead body is taken far away from the village and burned in a fire. The ashes are collected and put into hollow gourds. At the funeral, a shaman mixes the ashes with banana juice, and the closest family members drink the mixture. Drinking the ashes makes the spirit of the deceased live on with those who are still alive. During this ritual, women cry and men move together in a line, waving arrows and machetes and chanting. After the ritual, the mood becomes more peaceful, and everyone feasts again on meat and fruit. At the end of the yāimo, the hosts present the guests with many baskets full of food to eat on the way home.

GLOSSARY

ancestor: a person from whom one is descended

anthropologist: a scientist who studies human cultures

chant: a simple song that is usually sung in one tone

climate: the typical weather and weather patterns of a specific region

equator: an imaginary line that divides the earth into northern and southern halves

freshwater fish: fish that live in lakes or streams but not in the ocean

gourd: a fruit with a hard shell, which is often dried and used as a container after the fruit has been eaten

hatchet: a small ax with a hammerhead opposite the blade

humid: moist and sticky

immunity: the body's ability to fight off certain diseases

manioc: also called cassava; a very long and big root, native to tropical countries in the Americas, which is sometimes grated and pounded into flour

mercury: a metal that becomes liquid at room temperature. Mercury is poisonous and can harm people who eat, drink, or touch it.

missionaries: people who travel to foreign countries to teach others about and to convert them to their religion

reserve: a piece of land set aside for use by native peoples

river basin: the lands around a big river and all its tributaries

seminomadic: living in a fixed location for a while and traveling to different places at other times

shaman: a person who can communicate with the spirit world and use magic to heal sick people

taboo: forbidden for fear of sickness, harm, or death

tributary: a small river or stream that flows into a larger river or a lake

tropical rain forest: a forest of tall trees in a region of year-round warmth and plentiful rainfall

tropics: a broad band of warm regions to the north and south of the equator

FINDING OUT MORE

Books

Crespo, George. *How Iwariwa the Cayman Learned to Share.* New York: Clarion Books, 1995.

Johnson, Rebecca. *A Walk in the Rain Forest.* Minneapolis: Carohrhoda Books, Inc., 2001.

Kallen, Stuart A. *Life in the Amazon Rain Forest.* San Diego: Lucent Books, 1999.

Oldfield, Sara. *Rain Forests.* Minneapolis: Lerner Publications Company, 1995.

Peters, John F. *Life Among the Yanomami.* New York: Broadview Press, 1999.

Schwartz, David M., and Victor Englebert. *Yanomami: People of the Amazon.* New York: Lothrop Lee & Shepard Books, 1995.

Thomson, Ruth. *The Rainforest Indians.* New York: Children's Press, 1996.

Videos

Warriors of the Amazon. WGBH Video, 1996.

Yanomami, Keepers of the Flame. Video Project, 1992.

Websites

<http://www.mayastudies.org/yanomami.html>

<http://www.planeta.com/planeta/97/1197yanomani.html>

<http://www.ran.org>

<http://randomplace.com/yanomami/yano-art.htm>

<http://www.ukm.uio.no/etnografisk/utstillinger/midlertidig/yanomami/eng.htm>

Organizations

The Amazon Alliance
1367 Connecticut Avenue, N.W.
Suite 400
Washington, DC 20036-1860
(202) 785-3334
Website: <http://www.amazoncoalition.org>

Conservation International
1015 Eighteenth Street N.W.
Suite 1000
Washington, D.C. 20036
Website: <http://www.conservation.org>

INDEX

ABOUT THE AUTHOR

Raya Tahan is a writer based in Phoenix, Arizona. She has lived on three continents and has written on a wide variety of topics. Her work has appeared in newspapers, magazines, and Internet sites worldwide. She thanks Dr. Les Sponsel of the Department of Anthropology at the University of Hawaii, Dr. John F. Peters of the Department of Sociology and Anthropology at Wilfrid Laurier University, and Dr. Gale Goodwin-Gomez of the Department of Anthropology and Geography at Rhode Island College for their help with the preparation of this book.

PICTURE CREDITS

(B=bottom; C=center; F= far; I=inset; L=left; M=main; R=right; T=top)

ANA Press Agency: 19BR • Björn Klingwall: 25CL, 6-7M • John Maier Jr.: 36L, 38-39M • South American Pictures: 6CL, 7TR, 10-11M, 11TL • Still Pictures: 4, 8-9M, 9CR, 16-17M, 17CL, 20, 21BR, 25TR, 28, 32BL, 33B • Sue Cunningham Photography: 18CL, 11CL, 11BR, 15TL, 15CR, 17TR, 18-19M, 42CL, 41TL, 43TR, 46TL • Trip Photographic Library: 5BR, 8BL, 31B • Victor Englebert: cover, 1, 2TL, 3BR, 12-13M, 14-15M, 21CL, 22, 23TL, 23BR, 24-25M, 26, 27T, 27C, 29TR, 29CL, 31TL, 32CR, 34-35M, 35T, 37TL, 37CR, 37B, 38TR, 40R, 42-43M, 41BR, 44M, 45TL, 47BR, 48TL